# THE PURPOSE OF PAIN

# The Purpose of Pain

*How God Uses Pain to
Strengthen Your Resolve*

Tabitha Henton Lamb

# *Contents*

# Introduction

As believers, we've been created from the womb and predestined for something far greater than we can imagine. But our divine purpose can only be fulfilled when we are no longer operating as baby Christians feeding on milk. Spiritual maturity involves discovery of our purpose, and the shaping of our lives. Just as a child goes through many stages before he attains adulthood, God guides us through the ups and downs of life, especially the unpleasant side, to teach us many things. You cannot learn or grow in your Christian walk if everything is always pleasant!

Hope, faith and perseverance are core fruit of the spirit that enable you to wait on God with patient expectation, and the first path to finding your purpose in life is trusting in God completely. We learn to trust especially in uncertain times. Hope is born in uncertainty. Faith is born when hope is depleted, and perseverance gives us staying power in the midst of both. All come together to teach the believer different lessons in each phase.

As he falls and rises through pain, he begins to have a revelation of the enormity of his purpose. He learns how to translate painful experiences to strength through the help of the Holy Spirit. He learns how to encourage others and pursue his discovered purpose under the shadow of the Lord's wings (Psalm 91:1, 4).

This book is written primarily for believers to understand that there is a time and a season for everything. Just as there is a time for pleasurable experiences, there's also a stormy season marked out for everyone… now what we do during the storm determines the after story.

Would you let the storm crush you? Or will you let it draw you closer to God? Only then will you understand the reason behind the pain.

# UNDERSTANDING PAIN

Pain is basically any form of discomfort or hurt we experience, whether physical or emotional. Emotional pain is often a reaction to physical pain. Physical pain may go away with the help of proper medication or therapy, but emotional pain is tough to deal with and may do serious damage to the soul.

The seat of pain is the heart, which is the mind, the emotions, the conscience. As the core of our being, the heart is the place where decisions are made. It is the entrance of everything positive or negative, and helps us to interpret and deal with each experience.

I want you to understand that pain has a purpose and should not be seen as necessarily evil. We must first recognize that everything created under the sun by God is to teach us something. So let's establish some basic facts about pain. This listing will help you understand its intricacies, and lay a solid foundation for you to understand why it happens.

1. No believer is above pain. Jesus endured excruciating suffering at the cross, setting Himself as the perfect example for us to follow. If the Son of God could endure severe hardship, betrayal, brokenness from being abandoned, as His followers, we will all go through similar experiences. Did Jesus not say, *"If any man will come after me, let him deny himself, and take up his cross daily, and follow me"* (Luke 9:23)? And Hebrews 12:2 instructs us to look to Jesus, the author and finisher of our faith…who for the joy in the final reward endured the cross and surrendered all to the Father.

2. You can't have it all rosy! Cheer up! Our Father never promised us a bed of roses but many challenges. But He did promise us His protection. Did He not say ine not say inH Isaiah 43:2:

   *When thou passest through the waters, I will be with thee; and through the rivers, they shall not overflow thee: when thou walkest through the fire, thou shalt not be burned; neither shall the flame kindle upon thee.*

Fire clearly represents a turbulent time in our lives, turbulence perhaps in health, finances, career, personal relationships. Although fire hurts, it has purpose. Fire burns the old layers: it purifies. Your pain has come to transform you, to break the barriers of ego, pride, self sufficiency, so you have no option but to depend solely on Him.

If you carefully observe the heroes of the bible such as Abraham, Moses, Job and Paul, you'll come to appreciate the great odds they faced. It wasn't a smooth journey for any one of them, but through it they learned to trust God implicitly, and grew stronger after each painful episode.

We too will experience storms. We must learn to understand the times and seasons, and prepare our minds for the worst by praying for Grace to weather the storms. But always remember that even the most devastating storms do pass away!

Let's look at some of the heroes of our faith to gain from their experience.

# ABRAHAM

Although God had marked Abraham as father of all nations from the time of his calling, and gave him so many promises, Abraham was in pain. He had a desire, and that desire wasn't met. Ironically, he was extremely wealthy, but he and his wife were childless.

In the natural it was difficult to see how a man well into his eighties and a wife who was long past the age of child-bearing could possibly conceive. In a moment of weakness, he gave in to his wife's plan and took the maidservant Hagar as wife. A son Ishmael was born who would later be a thorn in the side to the people of Israel (Genesis 16).

But that was not God's plan. He was teaching Abraham a lesson in persistent faith to trust Him no matter how impossible it seemed. So in the fullness of time when Abraham was a hundred, he became the father of Isaac with Sarah. This was the son of promise to show forth God's miracle.

> *And being not weak in faith, he considered*
> *not his own body now dead, when he was*
> *about an hundred years old, neither yet*

*the deadness of Sarah's womb: He staggered not at the promise of God through unbelief; but was strong in faith, giving glory to God; And being fully persuaded that, what he had promised, he was able also to perform* (Romans 4:19-21).

## MOSES

Born as a child of Israel but raised in the courts as an Egyptian. Moses struggled with the problem of identity and guilt. He was hurt to see his people suffering, while he lived in luxury in the palace. One day while seeing a Hebrew being beaten by an Egyptian, he murdered the Egyptian There were other options he could have taken, but his pain gave rise to an anger problem. Moses thought he could escape from the crime but it became public and he was forced to run away into hiding (Exodus 2:11-22).

Sometimes when people are trying to escape from their pain, they turn to ungodly means which lands them in a far greater mess. From my reliable research, drug abuse, alcoholism, prostitution and other unhealthy lifestyles are forms of escapism. But they don't make the pain go away. They could give temporary gratification, but once the effects wear off, we're back to the bottom.

Moses also experienced pain when dealing with the Israelites by constantly being pressured by the people he'd been chosen to lead. Sometimes, the source of our pain could be from external pressure. Or it could be the voice of the flesh which always reminds us that we aren't good enough, or we aren't worthy of God's love. Sometimes we blame Him for our predicament.

Like Moses, we must always depend on God to work through our feelings.

# DAVID

Even as God's chosen leader over Israel, David was no stranger to conflict. Although he was anointed King of Israel by the prophet Samuel, he was tormented by the people's choice of king, Saul. Saul was jealous of David for his fame in killing Goliath, and hounded him for many years trying to kill him.

There were many other conflicts with his enemies including his own sons. No wonder, many of the psalms express David's cries to God and his struggles. Look at Psalm 142:4-6:

> *I looked on my right hand, and beheld, but there was no man that would know me: refuge failed me; no man cared for my soul. I cried unto thee, O LORD: I said, Thou art my refuge and my portion in the land of the living. Attend unto my cry; for I am brought very low: deliver me from my persecutors; for they are stronger than I.*

But, even though David struggled mightily with his faith, he never remained in a hopeless state for long, as he still concluded each psalm praising God and looking to Him in hope:

> *Bring my soul out of prison, that I may praise thy name: the righteous shall compass me about; for thou shalt deal bountifully with me* (verse 7).

# JOB

Perhaps no Bible character suffered more intensely than Job. Job had everything – a good family, a good name, and enormous wealth. But then Satan went to God and asked for permission to alter Job's good fortune to prove that Job would then curse God.

Then tragedy strikes and Job loses everything; his children, his wealth, his livestock, his crops, his health and even the relationship of his wife and friends.

And what does Job do? Not curse God, as Satan had thought. Instead, he praises His name.

> *Then Job arose, and rent his mantle, and shaved his head, and fell down upon the ground, and worshipped, And said, Naked came I out of my mother's womb, and naked shall I return thither: the LORD gave, and the LORD hath taken away; blessed be the name of the LORD. In all this Job sinned not, nor charged God foolishly (Job 1:20-22).*

All the same Job is completely transparent with God and questions His motive for his suffering, *"Is it good unto thee that thou shouldest oppress, that thou shouldest despise the work of thine hands, and shine upon the counsel of the wicked?"* (Job 10:3)

The moral of Job's story is: it's okay to question God or the reasons for why adversity strikes. But there's no need for us to stay there. The final picture is of Job having a revelation of the surpassing sovereignty of God and being humbled. He eventually repents and prays for his friends who misrepresented God to him.

## APOSTLE PAUL

Paul was a man who suffered greatly for the sake of the Gospel, but could still declare that nothing could separate him from the love of Christ. He'd not only grown accustomed to pain, but came to understand that sometimes pain is a pathway for discipline; it serves the purpose of correcting us, strengthening us, and helping us to grow spiritually.

Paul describes his ordeals below:

*…in labours more abundant, in stripes above measure, in prisons more frequent, in deaths oft. Of the Jews five times received I forty stripes save one. Thrice was I beaten with rods, once was I stoned, thrice I suffered shipwreck, a night and a day I have been in the deep; In journeyings often, in perils of waters, in perils of robbers, in perils by mine own countrymen, in perils by the heathen, in perils in the city, in perils in the wilderness, in perils in the sea, in perils among false brethren; In weariness and painfulness, in watchings often, in hunger and thirst, in fastings often, in cold and nakedness. Beside those things that are without, that which cometh upon me daily, the care of all the churches …(2 Corinthians 11:23-28).*

But he did not boast in overcoming all this on his own merits. His sole boast in his trials and in his victories was to know Christ and identify with His death:

*That I may know him, and the power of
his resurrection, and the fellowship of his
sufferings, being made conformable unto
his death... (Philippians 3:10).*

By the grace of God, Paul never gave up, but persisted in his mission to continue preaching the gospel to the Gentile world up to the time of his execution.

To sum up, none of these Bible characters had an easy life; but through pain they learned to trust God better and overcome adversity. Learning to kill the whining of the flesh, led them to know the greatness of Christ.

What can we add to this discussion about pain? Here are my insights:

1.  No one is immune to pain.

    Everyone is capable of feeling pain, even God. In Genesis, right about the time that God asked Noah to build the ark, the Bible records that God was so deeply troubled with man's sinfulness, He regretted creating man (Genesis 6:6)! If

God has such deep feelings, we can be assured that He can empathize with us too.

Sometimes, people pretend not to care or show what they are going through. But deep down they're hurting, and suppressing their emotions makes it worse. In the journey of understanding pain, and drawing strength from it, we must learn to channel our feelings to the right people. Above all, we have the Holy Spirit we can pour out our hearts to. We must invite Him into our hearts to heal us.

2.  We don't get to choose.

You can't choose the type of trial you want to handle! Disappointments, deaths, chronic illnesses, traumatic experiences do not always announce their arrival; they just happen! Take for example, losing a loved one to cancer or a bomb explosion! If we were asked to choose the kind of pain we'd prefer to experience, many people would go for the minimum – perhaps, a sting from a needle or an insect bite.

We can only react and learn lessons from each encounter.

3.  Time does not heal wounds.

    Contrary to the popular saying, if time heals old wounds, then we would have a world of peace and stability, not a world of traumatized victims who need constant therapy. But the opposite is what we see. Childhood trauma persists through adolescence and adulthood. It consumes the life of the victim and can destroy him.

    It is only the Spirit of God that heals completely. And that's what Jesus came for. He came to the earth to heal the broken hearted.

    *The Spirit of the Lord is upon me, because he hath anointed me to preach the gospel to the poor; he hath sent me to heal the brokenhearted, to preach deliverance to the captives, and recovering of sight to the blind, to set at liberty them that are bruised...(Luke 4:18)*

# PAIN AS A REFINER

We have come to know pain as any sort of mental or physical suffering or distress. Once we understand its purpose, we can choose to respond to it appropriately, for this will aid the true healing of the soul.

Just as we have been called to this great purpose of conformity to the image of Christ, we are also called to suffer with Christ. If we want to know Him and the power of His resurrection, then we will need to share in His suffering, becoming like Him in His death (Philippians 3:10). Not that our death is in any way redemptive, for only in Christ's death can we find salvation; yet, as joint heirs with Christ, if we willingly suffer with Him, we will also share in His glory (Romans 8:17).

However, we are often caught off guard by our sufferings, as though we ought to be exempt. We reason that since we are not condemned, why then should we continue to pay the price?

No doubt we hardly have all the answers for the mystery behind the pain we suffer especially as Christians. Only God can fathom the extent of evil in this world and the pain inflicted on its inhabitants. We wonder why believers who are acquitted from the responsibility must still receive the consequences deserved by sinners.

Let us go into this further. The Bible explains that suffering has a number of purposes connected with sanctification. One of them is the purification of our faith. Peter tells us that as gold is refined by fire, so is our faith perfected by hardship and trials; this will ultimately result in praise and glory and honor to Him (1Peter 1:7). Such an approach is borne out in our experience. When we suffer, we begin to know what really counts, and learn to trust only the things that last. We make fewer investments in the transitory and ephemeral.

Moreover, suffering helps us because it enables us to endure and gives us character. It strengthens our hope, the kind of hope that will never be shamed in the final outcome (Romans 5:4, 5). For this reason, we can be glad for the pain that God allows us to endure.

Not because there is anything good in pain but because there is a lesson for our faith!

In addition, pain renews our relationship with Christ. The major reason for Christian suffering is fellowship with Christ. We shouldn't be surprised at the trials that come our way but be glad that they mean we are communing with Christ in His sufferings (1Peter 4:12). It can even be said that we fill up what is lacking in Christ's afflictions, though not for redemptive purposes (Colossians1:24). It is easy to misunderstand such statements to mean we are somehow continuing in the unfinished business of Christ's passion. That theology isn't correct. Christ's suffering was once and for all! (Colossians 2:14; Hebrews 9:26), that is, the atoning value of his work on earth, culminating on the cross is sufficient and accomplished. Flagellants and others who believe they are participating in the atonement by their self-inflicted pain are far off the mark.

However, not all suffering is for atonement. The afflictions of Christ while on earth did not extend forward to include every hardship endured by His people. But when we suffer, it is because of Him (Mark 13:13). When Christians are persecuted, it is Christ who is the object (Acts 9:4-5). Although attacks on Christ during His lifetime were sufficient propitiation for God, His enemies were not satisfied. And so they continue to attack Him by attacking the church. His afflictions are now received by us.

So suffering increases intimacy with God.

Job, who endured unspeakable suffering said, "My ears had heard of You but now my eyes see You" (Job 42:5). Intimacy with God is often borne in the furnace of affliction. There's an opening of the soul that takes place in times of stress, and during the times of our greatest pain, we experience God at a deep and profound level.

Again, without suffering, we do not learn empathy. Suffering grants us the opportunity and strength to comfort others (2 Corinthians 1:3-5). Suffering gives us compassion for others who are hurting, enabling us to minister more effectively. Sufferers want to be around those who've shared their experience. They want people who have suffered to tell them there is hope. They are justifiably suspicious of people who appear to have lived a life of ease and only speak from textbook knowledge.

Those who've lost children can encourage those that are experiencing miscarriages. And when the sufferers see hope in the eyes of their comforter, they make God their point of reference.

Many of us usually compare our lives with those of the Bible characters who suffered greatly in life and we arrive at the conclusion that if God saw them through, then we can also overcome no matter what we face.

So suffering conforms us to God's image (Romans 8:29). We may be tempted to read these verses to say that God will bring good out of everything. While He can, and does redeem pain in our lives, these verses speak of being stamped with God's image through our suffering. If we are willing to sit still and let God work, we will find ourselves being transformed into the image of Jesus. Simply put, when we seek God through His word and prayer, we find Jesus. Remember, Jesus understands our pain because He, too, suffered.

Read the words of Psalm 22:1: *"My God, my God, why hast thou forsaken me? why art thou so far from helping me, and from the words of my roaring?"*

Did God abandon His Son in His hour of need? We find the answer three days later when God raised Him from the dead! Because of this promise, we have hope for our own future.

> *"My grace is sufficient for you, for my power is made perfect in weakness"* (2 Corinthians 12:9).

Also, while suffering pain, we should remember that life doesn't end there: it gets better. The whole creation groans with pain for an outcome (Romans 8:22). This sorrowful, broken world was subjected to futility by the same God who cursed the human race for its disobedience. And we suffer and groan along with it. World history doesn't end with death and futility. In fact, the whole creation will come to glory with us. The end is so unspeakably beautiful that our present sufferings are not worthy to compare with the glory to come. Physical death and suffering no longer have that dreaded finality they once had. Death of our self life is now the gateway to full communion with the Lord,

> *For you have died, and your life is hidden with Christ in God. When Christ who is your life appears, then you also will appear with him in glory* (Colossians 3:3-4).

We must learn and come to understand why pain enters our lives and to discover how God allows the process of it to entreat us. It is here we can dig our well deep to enable us to uncover and to achieve insight as to why a Sovereign God will make all this provision for us.

There are times He will set us in a place of aloneness, but this is not to be confused with a state of isolation, abandonment, or rejection. Unfortunately, this is the hardship our souls have to endure due to our limited knowledge and awareness of the process of pain.

There is a place He needs to reach deep inside of our soul that could only be accessed through an opening, the door of pain. You see, the area of hurt may have appeared to have been mended with a faulty scale, which must be revisited. For this is not the healing for which the blood and the stripes of Jesus paid the ultimate price. No, He must expose the temporary cosmetic healing and show us the real one. We must come to trust that He only wants His best for us, which is better than any outcome we can ever provide for ourselves to alleviate our pain.

His love does not drive us out as a castaway but draws us to Him for comfort. That is why we must flee from and abandon all familiar modes of self-protection. All proven forms of recovery and the false sense of repair we must come to identify and separate from us. We must come to depend solely upon Him for wholeness, complete healing, and full restoration.

Now we can understand the purpose and the goal of pain in life. The real motive and intent – it is to heal the right way – God's way. Empowered with this truth we must go in full throttle; we must not become paralyzed or fall in a trap or go back to the previous way of life because this particular type of hurt and or pain traps us in the wilderness to decay. The wilderness experience is meant for worship and exchange; instead, we made it a place of unnecessary wandering because of our complacency and complaints The result? Left to wander until death. We must seek more than the ability to blame or for an excuse to cover or to hide why a condition persists and recurs in repetitive cycles by different faces, scenarios and situations – but always the same outcome.

Let's go deep within ourselves in the light of Jesus, through the work of the precious Holy Spirit of God. Let us allow Him to pour in His healing to bring us to the outcome intended for us as believers in the stripes of Christ Jesus! Blessings to you!

# Chapter Three

# How To Process Pain With God's Help

# PART I

Do not lean on anything familiar or what you have come to understand about dealing with pain. "Only discern by the Spirit," says the Father. "Not by works but by My Spirit; do not judge by trauma but by My Spirit. You must remain outside of Trauma and in the Spirit."

Leaning on God is so important because just like any relationship He wants us to spend time with Him. Rely on Him. Bring Him into every single need. When life is overwhelming, it's just as important to lean on God as it is when life is easy.

He is our strength, our lifeline and the one who directs our steps. We need to lean on Him when we don't have the answers, when the mountain we need to be moved do not move, when the flood waters rise and there is no way out. We desperately need Him. We need His presence, and His peace. We need Him to be our refuge and our shield when we feel besieged by our enemies and just want to give up.

You may think that leaning on God makes you a weakling, a helpless dependent, but we must lean on Him in humility. Just as babies can't do without milk, we cannot do without God. So often, we trivialize who our God is. We think of Him as a friend, the pal we can walk right up to in everyday conversation – which isn't necessarily wrong. In many ways this is how we relate to God on a daily basis, but sometimes we can miss higher dimensions of God.

The highest quality of life one can have is a life in Christ. This is the original intent of God for man. We are not rebelling by design but rather by influence. The intent to rebel came from the rebel himself and it was by deception.

You must therefore guard and keep your heart: it belongs to God. Do not give it over to hurt, disappointment, unforgiveness, bitterness, or brokenness; it is His concern because He tells us to cast all our care on Him (1 Peter 5:7).

This is the real pressure test: in the mist of trials what you truly believe comes to the forefront. God is bigger; this is the answer to the test. This is the response to the test – walk it out as such.

Fight the poison – the toxicity of sin, the kingdom of darkness, carnality and the lust of the flesh the lust of the eyes, the pride of life.

*"Be still, and know that I am God,"* He says in Psalm 46:10. Be quiet in your voice, your thoughts, your habits, your heart. Be still and quiet your soul within you. Learn to move forward in faith and obedience instead of being paralyzed by trauma and fear.

It is vital to make Jesus the King of your heart, especially when the silent audible voice in your head begins to secretly control the quality of your life.

It is not yours to hold onto anything you have experienced. Release your whole life to God. Release everything since you were formed in the womb and agree with His purpose concerning you. This means all else must go, every hurt, pain, disappointment, failure, broken place, empty place, barren place, so your life can mirror what God had given you. You cannot mirror it back until you completely give up. You will be far from oppression because you have put on His righteousness:

*In righteousness shalt thou be established:*
*thou shalt be far from oppression; for thou*
*shalt not fear: and from terror; for it shall*
*not come near thee* (Isaiah 54:14).

See with your inner eyes and not your feelings and emotions. Do not lean on your own understanding based on your senses. Do not allow your mind to be fretted with fear or anxiety.

"Nothing anyone can do should drive you to do anything wrong before Me." This is when you are complete in Christ.

You must abandon the humanistic love of the world at all costs, as it forfeits the benefits of His perfect and unconditional love. You must love your neighbor as you love yourself. What a minimal cost in exchange for this unconditional love compared with the world's love, which must be earned, which is miserable, conditional and transitory!

If you truly believe God's love is perfect toward you, then all you require, He will do. This is the truth in opposition to distrust, hurt and pain and the need to self-protect. He will come in response to your prayer. The Lord will visit you in giving you bread – the truth of His word, you will see the things that entrapped your soul roll away like tumbleweed.

Shut down your spirit to everything but God. Seek out, if you must, the negative and bad because you need to be cleansed here and the memory erased. Only submit your spirit to God. Take authority and control over it, and offer it up to God. Your body has to become completely surrendered to Him.

Do not submit yourself to the evil circumstance or anything that is not of Christ. If He gives you peace, only walk in peace. If Joy, only walk in Joy. If Faith, cherish the measure of faith He has given to you, and let all else go. Anything not from God is not Him.

Stop running to fix the problems you did not create.

Stop micromanaging every area of your life because that leads to trauma.

Rest in God until the fear completely subsides and trembles at the presence of God. Take all the fragmented parts of you, and give them completely to God – your fragile heart, confused emotions, unfulfilled desires, all expectations, motives and agendas, options and last resorts, techniques and ploys. Apply grace to every person who has failed you in any of these areas.

He will take everything we surrender and fill it with His Holy Spirit. Jesus is the one and only person who will love us back to life. Jesus is the epitome of love – the love offering to the world.

You must empty out all the things that are still lingering in your heart; you must have no will at all concerning any given situation. God will never go against His Word. Look upon Jesus and He will heal you. You are looking for a resting place in the natural but true rest only comes in the spirit when your soul is at rest.

We exchange one form of fear for another, to only end up with an exchange of torment.

How you see pain determines your attitude to it. Let us redefine pain and give it a new name: Purpose Finder: this is what we will call pain from this point forward.

Just as resistance and pain strengthens and builds muscle in the natural, this same process is necessary. Pain and resistance are propellers for continued growth and development in life. We must learn to embrace it when it arrives at our door.

You must become sold on God to buy into this truth – there must be a resolution about you. It is here you will begin to feel strong and hardy on the inside. The pain and resistance training will prove to be a success: your muscle growth and development is solid.

It is here you have arrived with true faith and trust in God. You have no fear of hurt, harm, danger, ruin or destruction. It is a place you must arrive at in your soul – the inner man. This is the battle front and the battle ground.

Dismantle the fear, so that demonic spirit has no right, opportunity, or liberty to operate anymore. You must dismantle it all the way back to the roots of its inception.

A major root could be fear. Revisit all ungodly covenants that were made out of fear. You must release the fear behind the reason for the decisions you made in life. Repent and release that situation to God and trust Him to protect and to keep that area of concern.

One must yield to the work of the Holy Spirit constantly. This is what it means to yield, to consistently give Him the right of way in your life: to speak for you, to hear for you, to see for you, to desire for you, to love for you, to live for you, to think for you – it is not until this moment that one can trust his own life.

To trust in the Lord means every decision you make is done with Him in mind; it means to come to trust in His plan and not your plan. If the Lord says, "This is only a light affliction and you see trauma, it must mean you are in the wrong realm." We must learn to trust and come to believe His word at all costs.

We cannot allow our minds to be controlled with the toxicity of fear, to be paralyzed by this spirit against our will. It will cause us to do things we do not want to do. Spiritual discernment does not operate through the soulish realm. It operates in our born again spirit but never through our emotions. If the spirit of fear can get you emotional, you will not be aware of it, nor will you see the truth behind the ploy. The attack is always on the emotions to draw one into the realm of fear and out of the realm of the Spirit.

The devil does not want you to get to the place that God has assigned to you – the place of victory. Replace the threatening hand and face you see with His hand

and face and it is then you will have a clearer view. Do not live in fear of man and what he can do to you. Job agreed that *"the thing which I greatly feared has come upon me, and that which I was afraid of is come unto me"* (Job 3:25) because he was secretly dominated by fear and foreboding.

While fear may threaten to consume you, use it to propel you, ignite you, fuel you and drive you. Know that God will not allow a disruption before your time.

So be encouraged when tests and pain come because you know their purpose.

**Tests** are there to reveal our character and moral behavior. It is not until you are competent in the subject matter that you pass the test. Each man must be tested in the area of trustworthiness, so let the test become the wind beneath your kite to thrust it into the air.

**Pain** tells me *I am on the right track.* Another level, the next dimension is required –elevation if you will. The way to get there is through the eye of the storm. In that storm you will see Jesus in a far greater revelation than you've ever had before, until Satan is no longer present.

We must have a thirst, an all-consuming craving, a passion for the complete union with God and the fullness of the Spirit.[42]

*Chapter Four*

# HOW TO PROCESS PAIN WITH GOD'S HELP

# PART II

The Bible is clear on the importance of loving your enemy. It tells us to take no thought of an evil deed but, to do good to those who spitefully use you (Matthew 5:44). Set your focus on doing good and not on vengeance for the evil deed. Why is this so crucial? So that Satan will not take advantage of you, for we are not ignorant of his schemes to keep us walking in offense so he can gain access to our hearts and minds.

Jesus will rescue you; He will find you right where you are. He will assure you of a good outcome. He does not always reveal the process required to get to the outcome, which is why we must remain in faith and not fear. Do not allow the enemy to plague your mind. He will put distractions on you to engage in unnecessary warfare to drown out the voice of Truth, God's voice.

The test is in your words, and what is in your heart. Therefore, change what you believe in your heart, and change your confession to bring forth God's will in your situation. Stop giving your thoughts over to him to search out and nullify what God has given you; this is how your productivity is choked out, and why things never come to fruition.

So frame your life by the Word of God. *"Through faith we understand the worlds were framed by the Word of God, so that things which are seen were not made of things which do appear"* (Hebrews 11:3).

Your heart life, your love life, your desire life, your talk life, this is your retirement plan for your soul.

Storms show how strong your Faith is in God and what you truly believe. When you surrender all to Him, you open your life up to His protection. The enemy uses the power of suggestion to present various scenarios to you, but you can choose whether you will take the thought. You stay strong when you line up with the Truth, the Word of God. Do not change your theology because of your reality; change your reality to match up with your theology. Storms show a huge purpose; they show what you actually believe.

"Just love and I will fight all of your battles for you," says the Father. "I say unto you, count it all joy – when those you love persecute you and bring sorrows and troubles upon your heart." This is the reason, Jesus on the cross could cry, "Father, forgive them for they are clueless; do not charge their ignorance to them as their fault" (Luke 23:34). Love even more; love completely until the hurt is purified, and until your prayer conforms to the prayer of Jesus, "Father, forgive them."

> *Father, forgive them; have mercy upon them for they know not what they do. Nevertheless, I will serve You until I die. You are forever God and You reign supreme. Not my will but Your will be done. I humble myself and I relinquish what I should expect to receive from others. I release them, die to my rights and open myself to what You can do.*

Now that I know the truth, all I see is the cross. I have to forgive in order to fully experience all that it has for me. I now submit myself to God in all humility.

Settle in and take your time in this fight, for in your patience you will possess your soul. You will take full possession of it. Let patience have her perfect work that you may be entire, wanting nothing.

Perfect patience brings two blessings:

- Personal perfection in the knowledge of the gospel and the will of God
- Personal completeness in all the grace and gifts of God

Recognize when you are in a season of testing. Trust that God has set the parameters of the trial. There is only so far, He will allow it to go. Accept that you are being tested and tried for your own good. Psalm 119:71 says, *"It is good for me, that I have been afflicted; that I might learn thy statutes"* and Psalm 119:75 says, *"I know O LORD that thy judgments are right, and that thou in faithfulness hast afflicted me."*

Step into what He provides through Christ –into what His boundless might provide us just as Jesus, when He was being tested in the garden of Gethsemane, stepped into God's supernatural provision

*Who in the days of his flesh, when he had offered up prayers and supplications with strong crying and tears unto him that was able to save him from death, and was heard in that he feared; Though he were a Son, yet learned he obedience by the things which he suffered; And being made perfect, he became the author of eternal salvation unto all them that obey him...*
(Hebrews 5:7-9)

He was heard in that He feared – He had an awful sense of the wrath of God for the weight of our sin that He carried.

His human nature was ready to break under the heavy load. He would have sunk had He been forsaken at the point of His greatest need for help and comfort from God. But He was heard in this; He was supported under the agonies of death. He was carried through death.

By these sufferings He learned obedience. And though He was a Son, Christ learned further obedience by His suffering. Though He was never disobedient – He had never performed such an act of obedience unto death, even to the death of the cross.

Christ by His suffering was consecrated to His office by His own blood – by His suffering. He consummated that assignment of His office that was to be performed on earth to make reconciliation for our iniquity.

Through the "oil press" of Gethsemane – the place of agony of taking His cup of death on the cross – the flesh must be mortified and whipped into alignment with the will of God and kept in subjugation (Matthew 26:36-24). This is the only instance of agonized prayer because of the great battle between God and Satan over the final lap of the journey of Christ – and of all humankind.

This is how we are to handle spiritual warfare – in the spirit. Our battle is not with flesh and blood but with the demonic realm (Ephesians 6:12). Listen to His plea to the Father: *"O my Father, if it be possible, let this cup pass from me: nevertheless not as I will, but as thou wilt."*

And God heard Jesus' cry because of His godly fear (Hebrews 5:7). He did not save His Son from death because that would have gone against the redemption plan. But He did send an angel to strengthen Him to endure agony that no ordinary human strength could not endure: the bloody sweat, and the terrible struggle in the garden as He wrestled within Himself the horror of going to the cross.

Agony is great pain in a place of the utmost exertion to overcome all opposition to the goal. And Christ was in a life and death struggle in the garden; His prayer was one of great distress in wrestling with His own flesh and an act of submission.

Earlier He had told His disciples: *"The cup which My Father hath given me, shall I not drink it?* (John 18:11), referring to the Cross. And Isaiah 50:7 says His face was set like flint to describe His unwavering determination to persevere in the excruciating pain set before Him in the cross.

When faced with an insurmountable challenge, do away with your desires completely – all feelings, hopes, expectations, disappointments. Die to them as this will make the going smoother for you. Just see it all as the cup you must drink from the Father. Fail to see human faces from this point forward and chose to see only

Jesus. This is between you and God, the Father. If there are other faces involved, pray for all to disappear or get out of focus. This is the reality and it matches up with your theology to remain in this unswerving choice.

Release all of the human heart factors here: the guilt, the hurt, the expectations, the disappointment, the betrayal, the rejection, the infidelity, the abandonment, the separation and distinction, the treatment. Have no care for the heartless behavior – the actions or lack of them. All of the facets and phases of hurt and pain, whatever they maybe for you, release them all here. Do so because God has willed it, and this is the cup and the cross you must bear.

The feeling of being naked, uncovered and alone, body and soul is what you need and what can help you. Expect and desire as a woman in labor; lose it all in Him. There can be no disappointment if there is no expectation. Cursed is the man who puts his hope or trust, his expectation and security in man.

Evil does not have access to you in obedience. This is how one remains in the secret place: no self will; no need to disobey since you do not have any concern for any given matter, past present or future.

When you are suffering for purpose, everything will happen just the way it was supposed to – all of it! Everything! You are on the upside of this now. It was all allowed by God. "I had to bring you to a place in the Spirit, the place you had to get to; it is here you are learning obedience to My will. Do not allow yourself to succumb to human tendencies."

The vehicle of Man is his heart, flesh and mind. But the will of Christ broke through the human will, the human factor. He saw it for Himself through the eye of fear, the eye of pain, the eye of separation from the Father for the first time. When He saw this, He agonized in prayer in an attempt to change the will of God, to cause God to modify the plan. He wanted to impose the human factor to devise a different way to escape the anguish of His soul.

In one moment, the eye of the flesh, the eye of Satan, the eye of God, all three realms collided.

Yet, He learned obedience through what He suffered in the garden: *"Though he were a Son, yet learned he obedience by the things which he suffered..."* (Hebrews 5:8).

*"When He had spoken unto me, I was strengthened and said, let My Lord speak; for thou hast strength-ened me"* (Daniel 10:19b). Listen as He speaks and be strengthened.

# COMING OUT STRONG!

The human factor kicked in and became alive, for now God had insight into the internal workings of man, his heart, his mind, his feeling, his emotions, his fears, his will. It confirmed why He had to come down to see the wickedness of man, and why that knowledge was necessary for Jesus in flesh and bone to make intercession for us: to experience this as Man.

There is strength in sitting still and waiting on Him to speak to know the perfect will of God. As we wait, let us also be wise as serpents, and harmless as doves (Matthew 10:16).

What deception has the enemy blanketed over you so you don't see where he is hiding in your life? I present to you, strongholds and strongmen that prevent you from seeing Him for who He really is. Where is the enemy hiding in your thoughts – the thoughts that are valid and what you deem the truth? But now you must erase every memory, every thought, feeling or emotion. Why? Because they will come only through the carnal mind, the deceitful and wicked heart or out of the works of the flesh. Now you must only agree with God's word. You cannot trust your thoughts even if they seem true and valid. It is here you die to your mind and thoughts.

Here is where ascension begins for you. A new resident will take occupancy in your body, a visual death by crucifixion to life. He adjusts Himself in you so as to make room for His nature and character to form in you by way of the fruit of the Spirit.

Now is the time to empty yourself of all of what you call truth. You must not trust anything that you know or have come to learn; you must unlearn it so that you can come to the full knowledge of the Word of God. Do not trust what comes to your mind; only trust and allow what comes to your spirit. Reject what comes to the mind: it is of the carnal realm to keep you entrapped to secure its ways, its mindset, operations, opinions and thoughts. You must step outside of the arena to see the full exposure of its practices.

Be aware that the purpose of thoughts you are having is to keep you in some form of offense. The devil will try to re-enter a place you have surrendered. Do not allow him to regain a footing.

Say out aloud: "I forgive every one and reject every thought, feeling, reminder or memory lest Satan should get an advantage over me through offense to entrap my heart and keep me in bondage to something." Who or what does not matter, nor does it carry any weight. See the tactic and you will recognize the same ploy to regain possession of your heart and your thoughts.

It is not you; it is the devil who knows you will gain mastery over them in just a few more days. Do not look to others for the truth, the tactic was to distract you so you would not be led – typically you will not see it coming.

Demons do not require a response from you; just lift up Jesus. It is your character he is after to completely undermine. Give attention to each attack here; they have all been a blow to your character to discredit you so people will not hear you. You must learn to lean on the heart, spirit and mind that He will put on the inside of you. Every place of fear you will have to walk it out to take possession of it so that it can be offered up to God to sit as king. One must replace each fear with God – God will cause you to come through each one of them.

Hold your peace; allow the Lord to fight your battles for you, and the enemies will bow down in due season. Victory belongs to Him. You can do all things through Christ – to step into what His boundless might provides.

Until patience has her perfect work, where you are whole and lacking no good thing in you, it is necessary to take possession of your whole soul. It does not matter what the reason or way. His ways and His truth are not governed by circumstances. Do not flinch. It is here you trust God completely. It is here you gain absolute mastery and trust.

Consider these truths:

> Luke 21:19: … *in your patience possess ye your souls.*

By patient endurance you shall keep your souls in harmony with God and thus be saved.

> Luke 22:53: …*When I was daily with you in the temple, ye stretched forth no hands*

*against me: but this is your hour, and the power of darkness.*

John 18:4: *Jesus therefore, knowing all things that should come upon Him, went forth and said unto them, whom seek ye?*

Matthew 10:37: *He that loveth father or mother more than me is not worthy of me: and he that loveth son or daughter more than me is not worthy of me.*

In other words God is saying, "You cannot love anything more than Me; nothing can be more important than obedience to My will. He that loves Father or Mother more than Me is not worthy of Me."

See what happened in the garden when the band of people from the Pharisees came to arrest Jesus.

*Jesus therefore, knowing all things that should come upon him, went forth, and said unto them, Whom seek ye? They answered him, Jesus of Nazareth. Jesus saith unto them, I am he. And Judas also, which betrayed him, stood with them.*

> *As soon then as he had said unto them, I am he, they went backward, and fell to the ground* (John 18:4-6).

He could have killed them by His power if He had chosen to do so. This was a lesson that His accusers had no power over Him without His consent. He could have escaped if He had so desired and if it were not His time to go back to the Father. He spoke, not words of weakness and entreaty, but of authority.

"I give Myself to you voluntarily, but you must not hurt one of My disciples. I have already given you proof of My power over you. I will not use if on My behalf. For I lay down My life for My sheep, but I will use it if need be to protect My sheep."

And, certainly, it was certainly the power of Christ that protected them, especially after Peter began to use the sword. God permitted only the ear to be severed so as to cause another great miracle and further convince the soldiers that they were powerless to act without His consent.

"I have no fear, I lay no charge to My God, who is Holy and Righteous in all of His ways. He is the Truth;

it exists because of Him. You cannot trust or believe in someone else more than God. What they are capable of or can do, it is only because He has allowed it."

Who is Satan according to God? He is finite in his ability according to the design by which God created him – anything that he does is only because God permitted it, period. This is the truth that should govern your thought life, your heart life, your flesh.

The more you fall in love with Jesus and out of love with yourself you will find you can love others regardless of how they treat you.

No matter how real the thought may be in your mind, you cannot trust it because of the source, the carnal mind, no matter what feelings flood your heart and emotions, you cannot trust them; the source itself is deceitful and wicked. You cannot trust what your flesh wants you to know because it only wants to lead you to destruction by fulfilling its desires. This is the truth; one must govern one's heart mind and soul according by it. His tactic is to gain an advantage over you. Where is the blow or the attack? It's in the heart: identify it; cleanse it. Forgive everything in Christ. Part of the armor for the heart is forgiveness; it is vital to put it on daily.

"You have no security for yourself until you look to Me. So I ask you, how long will you allow the enemy to have access?" You must agree with Jesus concerning His intent for you. Life is all about winning, not being embarrassed or humiliated, shamed hurt, or disappointed. The pains of life, who is causing them, everything you think, see and discover, just give over to God.

"It cannot be about beating or getting the best of anyone. It must be complete surrender to Me. It can't be about what you can do but rather being led by My Spirit." You must come to a place of trust; you cannot afford to fall apart or to break down. It is not a possibility, nor is it an option. You must determine to go in a straight line to your purpose with nothing lost, whole and complete in Christ.

Step into Christ and stay there; don't come out. Change the battle plan. The fight is no longer to get in but to stay there. What is your strategy? Do not trust or allow the wrong thoughts regardless of their apparent validity. Do not trust the feelings or emotions of the heart; do not trust what the flesh wants to do.

Say with me: "I bring my body under subjection to do what I want it to do and that is to obey Christ." You must not attempt to take security in any of your usual methods: the only security one must have is in Christ.

Take the same stand as Job did:

*Though He slay me, yet will I trust in Him: I will maintain mine own ways before Him* (Job 13:15).

*Who is He that will plead for me? For now, if I hold my tongue, I shall give up the ghost* (Job 13:19).

*Withdraw thine hand from me: and let not thy dread make me afraid* (Job 13:21).

In closing, let us consider three men who went through trials. Which category do you fall into:

**Jesus** – His trial was sanctioned by God. Though at the last moment His flesh wanted another way out, He submitted to the will of the Father.

**Job** – he was offered up by God to the devil as a test of his loyalty. *"Many are the afflictions of the righteous: but the LORD delivereth him out of them all"* (Psalm 34:19). But he was persevered in his trials and God ultimately delivered Him and rewarded him.

I will wait until my change comes.

**Peter** – Satan desired to sift Peter. He did fall but God protected him.

Peter showed great boldness in trying to defend Jesus in the garden. He had vowed that he would never deny Jesus. He was the first one to draw his sword to fight back but also the first one to deny Jesus. Jesus warned them the flesh was weak but the spirit was willing. But in the end God raised him up to be His spokesman.

There is purpose in your pain. Pain is a propeller to center you in the purpose. It guarantees your bull's eye – so you aim with this purpose:

**Objective** - to be broken that you might be made whole

**Guidelines** - you must go it through God's way

**Intent** - to be useful for the kingdom

**Reason** - to be purified until the face of Jesus is reflected in you

**Outcome** – to establish Heaven as your eternal home

In all this, you will come to know God and to become aware of Satan and His devices. It is Satan that turns you away from speaking what God says to make you agree with the human heart and speak what you feel. You must discern regardless of whom it is that is turning you away. Discern the environment – do not open yourself up to anyone or any environment before you discern it.

# STANDING YOUR GROUND

It is here you will experience ascension above principalities and their power. You will be no longer beneath them but above them. For God dwells far above them in the highest heaven, the realm where there are no principalities. You are now seated with Christ Jesus, where only His power is in operation, where miracles happen daily (Ephesians 1:20-23). There is no shortage of the Power of God in His realm. The power of God is with Him and we must get in Him to experience His power.

We must give God the title deed to our soul. Offer it up to God to dress it and to keep it. Nothing in life can compare to Him. Nothing in this old heart, nothing in this old mind, nothing in these old fleshly components. Nothing can measure up or compare to.

The enemy will always target areas in your life that prove to be areas of vulnerability and weakness. Be careful of the need to explain yourself or the need for acceptance. You must define the areas of your thought life that you need to avoid.

"It was good for me that I was afflicted, for in that I came to the knowledge and understanding of Your laws and statues, I otherwise would not know nor would I have understanding of them," says Psalm 119:71.

Give attention to the details of your thought life. The enemy gains and seeks access to you here. You must drown out the negative by continuously focusing on Jesus, His word and His presence. Identify thoughts and beliefs that are fractured and in need of repair and mending.

You must take on an exchange with the value you give to your thoughts, feelings, pride and all knowledge you have. The facts you have to prove that you are right, the emotions, none of them can be more valuable to you than having Jesus. You must be willing to let it all go and give up all urges to justify yourself for the sake of knowing Him. Whatever has happened up to this point pales in the excellence of knowing Christ. It has all worked for a more eternal weight of Glory.

Forgive in Christ, for this is a sign that you know Him. Forgive every hurt, disappointment, feeling, thought, memory or emotion. You must let it all go – the ways of the world on the inside of you, the inner workings of your mind, heart, flesh – so that you may know Him..

Make a commitment that you will love Him out of desire only, not because of sorrow, hurt or pain.

Purpose in pain; count it all joy when you fall into diverse kinds of temptation, knowing that your faith is perfected as a result of trials (James 1:2-4). This is where patience becomes the master of your time; the end result is to regain possession of your soul in every area that has been demoralized. Just know all of your trials will be geared and tailor-made for this purpose: to get every part of your soul that does not belong to God, where He does not sit as Lord and King. We must pay attention to the trials; take none of them for granted; we must define them, investigate them, and study them.

Let's define the test or trial, what do they look like, what are its parts, what are its seasons and timeframes. It is a cycle:

The test

The trial

The purpose

Pain

Patience

When you align your thoughts with God, go through only the way He intended –the intended outcome with no damage, no residue. Strip from the devil the sting of pain in your heart. Pull an ambush on his schemes.

The areas of weakness in your life must be worked out and exercised to strengthen whatever particular area is being put through rigorous training. You would want to define that area. You endure the pain for the joy of accomplishing what you set out to do. He will literally take the sting out of that offense when you go through it the right way. When you submit to Him and surrender your will completely to Him, the pain will subside.

At this point you will receive a confirmation of His word, an understanding of why you went through it for a defining moment. You will find yourself on the other side of it. Now you can look and see your enemy has shifted into the shadows. He is no longer in front of you.

He is behind you now. Take one last look at the face of your enemy for you will see him no more. Today the Lord will fight for you. Say bye bye to your pain. No matter what happens, always remember to act out of the love of God. You will come to discover security in God when you put on Christ here, His strength, His ability, His boundless might. Put everything in the hands of God.

Identify the way the enemy can get to you; seal it up totally, anything to cause you to run back, to stop or to cause you to be hindered. Set your face like flint. Nothing will stop you or cause you to stop moving forward. The unsaved world around you will still entice and even pressurize you to go along with its wickedness. Sin is deceptive as it promises what it does not give, and gives what it never promised. Conquer deception with the truth of God's word. If you have specific temptations you frequently face, be sure to memorize scriptures that confront that sin directly. Also, rest in the knowledge that your satisfaction and joy come from God Himself:

> *Thou wilt shew me the path of life: in thy presence is fulness of joy; at thy right hand there are pleasures for evermore* (Psalm 16:11).

Fear is an area of weakness in your faith and it must be exposed, or made to come to the surface. This happens by circumstances or situations; the purpose is to allow you to see what is there to prove that belief is false evidence that only appears to be real. Then you must uproot it.

Sometimes a consecration is needed to bring the flesh under subjection so God can speak to us. The flesh will puff you up till you cannot do anything in the flesh with your words.

On this side of eternity, you will always be subject to temptations of some kind, for they are common to man. But know that temptation only works and succeeds when your heart is unprepared for it. *"But put ye on the Lord Jesus Christ, and make not provision for the flesh, to fulfil the lusts thereof"* (Romans 13:14). Take control of your fears, your weaknesses – don't let them get control of you.

Remember the Devil is not in control of the storms of life. In Jonah 1:4, it was the Lord who sent out a great wind into the sea, and there was a mighty tempest, which threatened to break the ship.

> *Then were the men exceedingly afraid, and said unto him. Why hast thou done this? For the men knew that he fled from the presence of the Lord, because he had told them... And he said unto them, Take me up, and cast me forth into the sea; so shall the sea be calm unto you: for I know that for my sake this great tempest is upon you…So, they took up Jonah and cast him forth into the sea: and the sea ceased from her raging* (Jonah 1:10, 12, 15).

Be mindful of the danger or harm this type of storm can do to others around you. The mariners lost all their possessions in trying to protect Jonah from a force they could not reckon with. They only escaped with their lives when they became aware of the truth because they forced him to confess.

Let's be like the men in the ship and cast that pain overboard. Let's forget the things that are behind and press on to those things that are before so we can move forward (Philippians 3:13).

Jabez whose name means "he makes sorrowful" was given that name by his mom probably due to the pain of childbirth. That memory was more valuable to her than her future and the future of her seed. But Jabez decided to rise up and pray to God to remove that evil from him and bless him instead:

> *Oh that thou wouldest bless me indeed, and enlarge my coast, and that thine hand might be with me, and that thou wouldest keep me from evil, that it may not grieve me! And God granted him that which he requested* (1 Chronicles 4:10).

Naomi said to her friends on returning to Bethlehem after the untimely deaths of her husband and two sons in Moab, "*Call me not Naomi, call me Mara: for the Almighty hath dealt very bitterly with me*" (Ruth 1:20). She tried to send her daughters-in-law away because she knew there was no possibility of a future for the two young widows, and all she could think of was to put herself at the mercy of the law concerning a widow; that was the only hope she saw for her. The burden of anything more was more that she could bear.

Because of the famine at the time in Bethlehem, she had left her country in high hopes of a better life in Moab, (girl, he got a new job, we are moving up in the world!). Now she must return and face the same people that she left behind in humiliation. "Call me not who I used to be – not anymore!" So she renamed herself for this season in her life, because her life was even more bitter with the loss of her husband and sons. She was now at the mercy of the goodwill of the system that she was once above.

But all this was about to change. It was not until she saw Boaz's great favor to Ruth that she began to see the provision God had in place for her future and her daughter-in-law. Not just provision but transition to a whole new destiny, for she became the grandmother of a son who would be in the lineage of David, and from David, the Messiah. The enemy wanted her to send her back just to receive charity and prompted her to name herself "Bitter." But God intended for her and Ruth to walk into a glorious future.

# Chapter Seven

# THE POWER OF THE TONGUE

The lessons of Jabez and Naomi teach us not to speak any words the enemy wants you to prophesy over yourself in order to gain a foothold on you. No negative words! Continue to cast them down.

Listen to what God is saying, "I will continue to strengthen you that your inner man might be strong. Your words start with your thoughts. The dominant thoughts in your mind will create your outer world. What you set your mind on will determine your future. Your thoughts and words are conduits of your reality."

Even when we can't choose or control our circumstances, we can still decide how to respond to them. Apostle Paul was in prison when he wrote, *"Rejoice in the Lord always"* (Philippians 4:4) and indeed that letter written in the dark dank cell is one of the most joyful of his epistles.

As Jesus said, our words are Spirit and life:

*It is the spirit that quickeneth; the flesh profiteth nothing: the words that I speak unto you, they are spirit, and they are life* (John 6:63).

The trouble is we don't always recognize when we're speaking negative words over ourselves when we constantly think and say things like, "I'm not good enough," "Why am I so unlucky?" "Everything is stacked against me."

We settle for defeat when, with a few attitude adjustments, we could open the door to amazing possibilities. The worst part of negative self-talk is that we don't just limit ourselves: we limit God. As His redeemed children, within each of us is the power to think better, talk better, and do better.

When we speak negative words over our life, we are building strongholds. A stronghold is like a fortress you built around you based on a false identity. It could be caused by pride or arrogance or deception, but it obscures the real you. That is sufficient ground for the enemy to enter and take possession of.

We must not only learn the importance of steering clear of negative thoughts and words. There is also another factor to be acutely aware of when speaking idle words.

Matthew 12:36-37:

*But I say unto you, That every idle word that men shall speak, they shall give account thereof in the day of judgment.*

Matthew 12:37:

*For by thy words thou shalt be justified, and by thy words thou shalt be condemned.*

Ultimately, we will have to give an account of idle words when they are used as a misuse of power. Words are indeed a creative force, for we saw that it is by the word of God the worlds were framed into existence. If things were called into existence by the word, the reverse is also true. We can negate good things by our words, sometimes through our idle musings. Without much thought, we can tear down businesses, people, even ministers of the gospel by our loose talk.

Even if we are passive listeners of gossip, we allow our soul to be contaminated. As Proverbs 18:8 says, *"The words of a talebearer are as wounds, and they go down into the innermost parts of the belly."*

The enemy often uses the power of suggestion to create doubt or confusion. "Did God say you cannot eat of all the fruit in the garden?" he said to Eve, opening a conversation aimed at casting aspersions at God and undermining their relationship with Him. Eve could have chosen to deny those innuendos and move on, or not to respond at all. The moment she engaged, she was snared by the crafty foe.

Like Eve, when thoughts are presented to you, you will have to choose whether or not you will take the bait. It could be some juicy morsel about a friend or an attempt to smear the reputation of an important figure. Do not participate if you do not know where all this is heading. In the end, you damage your delicate soul.

We must come to a clear understanding about the human mind outside of the mind of Christ. The unrenewed human mind is carnal and its purpose is enmity towards God. It is not subject to the law of God, neither indeed can it be because it does not want to live by God's moral and spiritual laws. It seeks to live by its own rights and its own way (Romans 8:7). So do not give it a chance to rear its head.

Proverbs 18:21 says: *"Death and life are in the power of the tongue: and they that love it shall eat the fruit thereof."* Our words have power, and we can speak positive words of light or negative words of darkness. Those who speak with caution will be rewarded. Those who speak recklessly will suffer the consequences of their words.

The difference between speaking death or life over a situation is so dramatically illustrated in Jesus cursing the fig tree for giving the appearance of fruitfulness when it was barren. From a distance, its leafy foliage promised fruitfulness but when Jesus approached it closer, He found it was fruitless.

*"No man eat fruit of thee hereafter for ever,"* He pronounced over it. *"And in the morning, as they passed by, they saw the fig tree dried up from the roots"* (Matthew 11:14, 20).

These may seem like damning words for such a seemingly trivial event but I believe the Holy Spirit wants to convey a much deeper message. The barren fig tree speaks of subtle deception, of outward appearance and inner hollowness, of pretending to be good and wholesome when inwardly a thing is rotten to the core. Of even greater significance is that the fig tree represents the chosen ones, the people of God. If the elect can lead others into deception, what a great calamity indeed!

What is the Holy Spirit saying in our global society when deception is so rampant? How is this relevant to the words we hear and speak out, and the conversations we participate in?

I believe this is the message of the hour.

Do not judge things by their appearance but test all things. What appears good may be laced with evil. This is especially so with the media which may be broadcasting a false message across the board because they are controlled by the same sinister agenda. Do not accept all news touted by the media or be pressurized by your peers to believe what the world accepts as the truth. Again, discern the spirit behind the platforms, for many are agents of spiritual wickedness in high places.

Be especially cautious in your communication on social media because this is Satan's hotbed of rumor-mongering, innuendo, and allegations which cause confusion, divisions and fear. Be wary of participating in such loose talk, for you will be judged for contaminating the souls of a wide audience, especially the young.

Exercise caution in any chat group as well because of the spiritual energy in them. Even if they purport to be Christian, the divergent opinions within the group may undermine the purity of your calling and may nullify your prayers. What is the point of praying in one direction when it is negated by people within the group? Do not get sucked into such a community for the appearance of unity.

In conclusion, my brothers and sisters, let our speech be always with grace, *seasoned with salt*, that we may know how we ought to answer every man (Colossians 4:6). When you are confronted with a sea of bad news which undermines all you stand for, your strategy must be to act in the opposite direction. Like Jesus did to the fig tree, declare death to the corruptions of this age. And like Ezekiel, declare life to the dry bones waiting to be revived (Ezekiel 37:4-8).

So get into agreement with like-minded prayer partners:

Declare good news to the poor, healing for the brokenhearted, deliverance for the captives (Isaiah 61:1-3).

Nullify the effects of toxic substances that many have taken through ignorance by declaring Mark 16:18 over them.

Declare the downfall of the media and all platforms that propagate lies.

Pray for God's truth to emerge to set people free.

Declare protection and safety to the remnant who stand for God's truth.

Pray for the good of the land and for all the nations of the earth, for the government of the nations is upon God's shoulder (Isaiah 9:6).

Declare God's will on earth as it is in heaven (Matthew 6:10).

I will now invite the Lord to have the last word: "Do not allow the enemy to plague your mind.

Distractions cause you to engage in warfare you otherwise would not have entered into. To drown out the voice of truth in your life, the test is in your words and what is in your heart. Change what you believe in your heart, and change your confession to bring forth what I will for your life!"

# Conclusion

Every individual God used mightily throughout Scripture went through seasons of hardship. Moses had to flee the Egyptians who wanted to kill him, Elijah had Jezebel seeking his death, Queen Esther risked her life to save the Jewish people, our Savior was beaten and crucified and all but one of His disciples were martyred for their commitment to Him.

So, believer, examine yourself this day. Confirm any pain or suffering you find. Question God if you must, but know He has a purpose planted in you that announces His expressed confidence that you can bear the burden He has brought or allowed to be brought to you. Pray for His guidance. Read His glorious word. Watch long and closely because the revelation is not always immediate and obvious. If you need help, find a church that preaches and teaches the Word where you can learn more about God's purpose for your life.